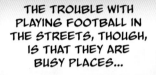

THE TROUBLE WITH PLAYING FOOTBALL IN THE STREETS, THOUGH, IS THAT THEY ARE BUSY PLACES...

7

CHAPTER TWO

WONDER BOY

Cristiano lived in a small, crowded tin shack with his parents and two older sisters, Katia and Elmo, and his older brother, Hugo. It was in a poor part of town — the family had little money — but it was home. Cristiano spent all of his time outside playing football.

One day, when Cristiano arrived home from school, he was confronted by Hugo and cousin Nuno.

'Oh no. I must be in trouble,' he thought.

'You're coming with us, Cris,' said Hugo.

'Why? What have I done?' asked Cristiano.

'Just do as you're told,' replied Hugo.

Hugo and Nuno walked off and Cristiano followed after them slowly.

Suddenly, Cristiano knew where they were going. He'd been this way before with his dad. The road they were on led to only one place: Andorinha Football Club. Hugo and Nuno both played for youth teams at the club.

When they reached the gates, Hugo turned to Cristiano and said: 'You're joining the junior team.'

At first, Cristiano felt shy. All the other boys were older and bigger than he was. But, slowly, he got used to it. Training was very different to kickabouts in the street! There were cones to run round, and everyone had to do exercises.

Soon, Cristiano established himself in the boys' first team. He played 7-a-side games on Saturdays and 11-a-side games on Sundays. Everyone could see that he was special; not only did he have skill, but he was always, always practising! At every match, his dad was there to encourage him.

One day, a couple of years after Cristiano started playing for the Andorinha junior team, the youth-team coach at Madeira's top professional club, CD Nacional, was having a meeting with his scouts.

'I saw this kid playing for Andorinha,' one of the scouts told the coach. 'He's a bit of a wonder boy.'

'I'll go over there and take a look at him,' said the coach.

At the next Andorinha match, the coach watched as the 'wonder boy' outplayed everyone else on the pitch. Straight after the match, he signed Cristiano as a CD Nacional junior player.

CHAPTER THREE
HOMESICK

For two years, Cristiano played in the junior teams at CD Nacional. They called him 'little bee', because he was always darting here, there and everywhere on the pitch. Soon, the big professional clubs in Portugal heard about Cristiano's talent. They came to Madeira to see him play, but their verdict was always the same:

HE MIGHT PLAY LIKE A BEE, BUT HE LOOKS LIKE A NOODLE. HE NEEDS TO BUILD UP HIS STRENGTH.

YEAH, THE KID IS GOOD, BUT HE'S SO SKINNY.

'Cris, you've got the makings of a top player,' his father told him. 'But you've got to eat more.'

'I don't have time,' Cristiano protested.

'What did you have for lunch?'

'A yoghurt.'

Cristiano's mum made him lunches of fish and meat. Gradually, he grew bigger.

When he was twelve, Cristiano signed for one of Portugal's top professional teams, Sporting Lisbon. His transfer fee was just £1,500.

From the moment the plane took off, Cristiano felt unhappy. He'd never been away from home before and here he was flying 970 kilometres to go and live in a large city with people who weren't his family.

There were about 20 boys in the Sporting Lisbon Youth set up, most of whom were at least two years older than Cristiano. People from Madeira speak Portuguese with a strong accent. Cristiano struggled to make himself understood. He felt like a stranger in an alien land.

At night, Cristiano would lie awake in bed, homesick for his friends and family.

DAD AND THE OTHERS WANT ME TO DO WELL, BUT IS IT WORTH BEING THIS UNHAPPY? JUST TO GET THE CHANCE OF BECOMING A PROFESSIONAL FOOTBALLER...

Cristiano had no parents or older brother and sisters to look after him now. He had to do his own washing ...

and ironing ...

and look after himself.

Gradually, he got used to life in Lisbon. He watched Sporting Lisbon first team play every match, earning extra money as a ball boy. He became captain of the Under 15s and enjoyed the challenge of encouraging and inspiring his teammates. Then, during one match he suddenly felt a dull pain in his chest. His heart was pounding. He had to fight to get his breath.

Cristiano couldn't run for the ball. He stood gasping with his hands on his knees.

Another member of the team saw that he was in trouble and kicked the ball into touch.

The medics ran onto the pitch and took one look at Cristiano. 'You're coming off,' they told him. 'We don't quite know what's wrong, but what ever it is, it looks serious.'

CHAPTER FOUR
UNITED COME CALLING

It was serious.

'You've got a racing heart,' explained the doctor who examined Cristiano.

'Is that bad then?' asked Cristiano. It sounded like a racing heart might be a good thing for a footballer if it meant it helped you race down the wing.

'Bad?' the doctor said, gravely. 'For a professional footballer, it can be fatal.'

Cristiano felt very scared. 'I could've died out there,' he thought. Then another dreadful thought struck him: 'Will I be able to play football again?' he asked the doctor.

'You'll need an operation, but you should be fine,' the doctor told him.

Cristiano was operated on straight away, using laser surgery.

It was three months before he was well enough to play football again.

When Cristiano finally returned to full match fitness, there was no stopping him. He broke a club record by becoming the first player to play for Sporting Lisbon's under-16, under-17, under-18, B team, and first team, all in one season!

By now, scouts from the big European clubs were beginning to take notice of the talented teenager.

One day, Cristiano's agent got a call from London. 'Hi, I'm calling from Arsenal Football Club. Would your lad

Ronaldo like to spend a weekend in London? Arsene Wenger would like to meet him and show him the set up we've got here.'

Cristiano and his mum had a great time in London. He liked the look of Arsenal Football Club. They all seemed a friendly bunch.

'I look forward to seeing you in an Arsenal shirt very soon,' Arsene Wenger told Cristiano. Liverpool, Barcelona and Real Madrid were also interested in the young winger.

At the start of the 2003 season, Sporting Lisbon played a pre-season friendly against Manchester United. Cristiano was in the Sporting Lisbon team. He played a blinder. He gave the United full back John O'Shea such a tough time, that the defender was forced off at half time with a migraine.

After the match...
WHERE'S THE BOSS GOT TO? IF HE'S MUCH LONGER, WE'LL MISS OUR FLIGHT.
YOU MIGHT AS WELL GET OFF THE BUS AND STRETCH YOUR LEGS, LADS. WE COULD BE HERE A WHILE.
WHY'S THAT?
MR FERGUSON HAS GONE TO SEE SPORTING'S CHIEF EXECUTIVE...
HE SAYS WE'RE NOT GOING ANYWHERE UNTIL HE'S SIGNED THAT KID RONALDO!

CHAPTER FIVE
THE £12 MILLION TEENAGER

Cristiano got out of the taxi and stared up open-mouthed at the huge building in front of him: Old Trafford, home of Manchester United Football Club.

Sir Alex Ferguson had indeed signed Cristiano Ronaldo from Sporting Lisbon. The fee? A cool £12.24 million; a record for a player of Cristiano's age.

Cristiano and his mother were visiting Manchester for the first time, to look at the club and the city. They also wanted to discuss when the teenager would join Manchester United. Cristiano expected to stay on at Sporting Lisbon for the new season, as a loan player. After all, he was only eighteen.

Sir Alex Ferguson sat down with Cristiano and his mother. They were in one of the executive boxes that overlook the United pitch.

'So, are you looking forward to becoming a Manchester United player?' Sir Alex Ferguson asked.

Cristiano nodded, shyly.

'We've got a nice house where you and your mum can stay until you find somewhere permanent,' Sir Alex added.

Cristiano frowned. 'A house? The hotel will be fine for tonight. We fly back to Portugal tomorrow.'

Sir Alex Ferguson raised his eyebrows in surprise. 'Flying back to Portugal?' He shook his head. 'Sorry son, I thought you'd been told. There's been a change of plan. You're not going back on loan to Sporting Lisbon. You're going to start training with the Manchester United squad in the morning.'

Cristiano's mind was in a whirl. He'd expected a whole year to prepare for his move to Manchester. Instead, he had less than twenty four hours!

That afternoon, Sir Alex Ferguson presented Cristiano with his United shirt. Cristiano thought it would be a number 32 shirt, his number in the Sporting Lisbon squad, but there was a number 7 on the back.

Cristiano gulped. Number 7 was worn by Manchester United legends. He was just a teenager. How could he follow in the footsteps of such footballing giants as Beckham, Cantona and Best?

CHAPTER SIX
TOUGH TIMES

Of course, the Manchester United players knew just how good Cristiano was; they'd played against him in Lisbon. The fans, though, were less than impressed. How could an unknown Portuguese teenager ever possibly replace the great David Beckham? What was Sir Alex Ferguson thinking of, spending £12 million on a kid? Opposition fans also mocked the new signing.

It was a difficult start for Cristiano, but in his tenth match for United he scored against Portsmouth: his first goal in the famous number 7 shirt.

Then in the 2004 Cup Final, Cristiano's stunning header opened the scoring in United's 3—0 thrashing of Millwall.

It was the first time Cristiano had ever been in a team that had won a trophy. But he still didn't look like a player worth £12 million. During the 2004—5 season he played 33 matches for United and scored just five goals. His teammates, some of whom remembered his blistering performance against United in Lisbon, wondered if he would ever find his form. The fans hadn't warmed to him either. 'We're paying him film-star wages and he can't manage more than five goals a season?' they moaned.

Cristiano put his wages to good use, though, helping his family. By the start of the 2005—6 season, his dad was seriously ill. Cristiano paid for him to have treatment at a London clinic.

'The doctors in the clinic are the best,' Cristiano told his dad. 'They'll soon have you on the mend.'

But Cristiano's father did not get any better. Sadly his condition worsened, and in September 2005 he died. Cristiano was heartbroken.

'I thought the money I had to pay for him to be treated in a top clinic would help save his life,' Cristiano told his sister, Katia. 'But it didn't.'

Katia shook her head, sadly. 'Dad was the one who got you started in football, wasn't he?'

Cristiano nodded. 'He took me to training, gave me advice about my game, cheered me up when things hadn't gone so well on the pitch. He inspired me to become a professional footballer.'

Katia nodded. 'He always believed that you could become a footballing legend,' she said, quietly.

CHAPTER SEVEN

LEGEND

For Cristiano though, becoming a legend seemed like a distant dream.

In a match between Portugal and England at the 2006 World Cup, Cristiano clashed with Wayne Rooney. The England striker received a red card, and was sent off. The supporters blamed the Portuguese striker. It seemed that Cristiano Ronaldo would never win over the Manchester United fans.

The 2006–7 season started quietly for Cristiano, but by February 2007 Manchester United were on course to claim their first League title for four years. They needed to win at Fulham to maintain their title push, but the game was fast heading towards a 1–1 draw.

Manchester United 1-1 Fulham FC
88 minutes
THERE'S JUST TWO MINUTES OF NORMAL TIME. MAN UTD HAVE THE BALL ON THE HALF WAY LINE WITH RONALDO.
HE'S PAST ONE!

Three months later, Ronaldo scored the only goal in the Manchester derby; a goal and a win that meant United were League Champions. This was the Cristiano Ronaldo his teammates remembered from that match at Sporting Lisbon.

The following season, Cristiano scored an astonishing 31 goals as United won the Premier League title again.

During the 2008—9 season, Cristiano scored 26 goals in all competitions as Manchester United won the Premier League title for the third year running. When the team ran round the Old Trafford pitch on their lap of honour, the terraces rocked to the sound of the fans' latest chant:

As Cristiano waved to the crowd, the memories of his father encouraging him as a youngster came flooding back.

And with the crowd's chanting of his name ringing in his ears, he knew for sure that he had finally taken his place alongside George Best, Eric Cantona and David Beckham.

He had become a Manchester United legend.

On 10th May 2009, Cristiano Ronaldo scored the first goal in United's 2–0 win against their old rivals Manchester City. It was his last ever goal for the club.

At the start of the 2009–10 season, he joined Real Madrid for a world-record transfer fee of £80 million.

Since then, he has become a favourite at Real's home ground, the Santiago

Bernabeu Stadium. In 2014, he scored
as Real beat Atlético in the Champions
League Final to win the European Cup
for a record tenth time — La Decima.

CHAPTER EIGHT
EURO 2016

Cristiano had been a member of the Portugal team since he was eighteen, and had been their captain since 2006.

At the 2016 European Championships, Portugal struggled through to a semi-final clash with Wales.

Fifty minutes into the match, Cristiano rose magnificently to fire a bullet header into the Wales net.

'It's Ronaldo!' the commentator yelled. 'An unstoppable header!'

Portugal went on to win 2—0, earning themselves a place in the final against the hosts, France.

The French started the match at a furious pace. In the eighth minute, France's Dimitri Payet went in with a hard tackle on Cristiano and he went down, clutching his knee.

'Aargh!'

Cristiano limped off. Twice, he attempted to come back on the pitch, but eventually, after 25 minutes, he was stretchered off.

'It's all over for Ronaldo!' the TV commentators said.

They were wrong. Cristiano, with his knee heavily bandaged, hobbled up and down the touchline, urging his side on.

'Listen guys,' he told them at half time. 'You can do it! Stay together and fight for it!'

And Portugal did fight for it. With Cristiano roaring his team on from the touchline, they won the match 1–0 in extra time.

It was Portugal's first ever trophy. Cristiano was a hero now, not just for his club, but for his country, too.

SPORTING 🏆 HEROES

FACT FILE

Full name: Cristiano Ronaldo dos Santos Aveiro

Date of birth: 5th February 1985

Place of Birth: Funchal, Madeira, Portugal

Height: 1.85m (6ft 1in)

GLOSSARY

blinder — to play well (during a match) with lots of skill

form — a measure of how a sportsperson has performed recently

friendly match — a non-competitive match, often used to test different formations and players

full back — a defender playing on the left or right side of the pitch

into touch — when the ball goes out of play (over a touchline)

La Decima — Spanish for 'the tenth'

winger — an attacking player positioned on the far left or right

CAREER

Trophies won at Manchester United

Premier League	2006–07, 2007–08, 2008–09
FA Cup	2003–04
League Cup	2005–06, 2008–09
FA Community Shield	2007
UEFA Champions League	2007–08
FIFA Club World Cup	2008

Trophies won at Real Madrid

La Liga	2011–12
Copa del Ray	2010–11, 2013–14
Supercopa de España	2012
UEFA Champions League	2013–14, 2015–16
UEFA Super Cup	2014, 2016
FIFA Club World Cup	2014, 2016

Top Individual Honours

Ballon d'Or	2008
FIFA Ballon d'Or	2013, 2014, 2016
FIFPro World Player of the Year (first Premier League player to receive this award)	2008
European Golden Shoe	2007–08, 2010–11, 2013–14, 2014–15

Records

The Most Expensive Footballer in History	2009–13
Most International Goals in a Year* (25)	2012

First footballer to reach 40 goals in a
professional league for two consecutive seasons

Most goals scored in the UEFA Champions League (95)

*Shared with Vivian Woodward and Lionel Messi

SPORTING 🏆 HEROES

'Jamie! Keep the ball closer to your feet. Closer!'

The coach was instructing Jamie how to dribble the ball through a line of cones. Being a schoolboy apprentice wasn't just about playing football matches, there was training to do as well. Dribbling, sprinting, shooting at goal; they were all part of the young footballer's routine.

But Jamie didn't mind. He loved every minute of it...

CONTINUE READING
JAMIE VARDY'S
AMAZING STORY IN...